IT'S TIME TO EAT STROMBOLI

It's Time to Eat STROMBOLI

Walter the Educator

Silent King Books
A WhichHead Entertainment Imprint

Copyright © 2024 by Walter the Educator

All rights reserved. No part of this book may be reproduced in any manner whatsoever without written per- mission except in the case of brief quotations embodied in critical articles and reviews.

First Printing, 2024

Disclaimer

This book is a literary work; the story is not about specific persons, locations, situations, and/or circumstances unless mentioned in a historical context. Any resemblance to real persons, locations, situations, and/or circumstances is coincidental. This book is for entertainment and informational purposes only. The author and publisher offer this information without warranties expressed or implied. No matter the grounds, neither the author nor the publisher will be accountable for any losses, injuries, or other damages caused by the reader's use of this book. The use of this book acknowledges an understanding and acceptance of this disclaimer.

It's Time to Eat STROMBOLI is a collectible early learning book by Walter the Educator suitable for all ages belonging to Walter the Educator's Time to Eat Book Series. Collect more books at WaltertheEducator.com

USE THE EXTRA SPACE TO TAKE NOTES AND DOCUMENT YOUR MEMORIES

STROMBOLI

Roll up, roll up, it's Stromboli time,

It's Time to Eat
Stromboli

A treat so tasty, it's simply sublime.

Cheesy, meaty, with dough wrapped tight,

It's warm and yummy, a dinner delight!

Inside the crust, there's a hidden surprise,

Pepperoni and sauce make big happy eyes.

Melted mozzarella and spices so fine,

Every bite feels like a treasure to find.

Cut it in slices, see the swirls unfold,

With colors of red, white, and gold.

Dip it in marinara, oh, what a taste,

No single crumb should go to waste!

It's crispy outside, so soft within,

Where does the flavor even begin?

Is it the cheese? Or the spices galore?

Each bite just makes us want even more!

It's Time to Eat
Stromboli

Stromboli's a bundle of tasty delight,

Perfect for lunch or dinner tonight.

You can hold it in your hands or use a fork,

It's loved by all, from south to north.

Spinach and veggies or sausage and ham,

Stromboli's the meal that says, "Here I am!"

You can mix it up, or keep it the same,

It's the kind of food that always feels game.

Make it together, roll out the dough,

Spread the fillings, then fold it just so.

Pop it in the oven to bake it just right,

Soon it's Stromboli, what a delight!

Invite your friends, call them to eat,

Stromboli's the food that can't be beat.

Big slices for grown-ups, small ones for kids,

It's Time to Eat
Stromboli

It's a family meal, no one forbids!

Hot and savory, it fills the air,

Stromboli's a dinner that shows you care.

So gather around and take a seat,

It's time for Stromboli, what a treat!

So next time you're hungry, you know what to do,

Stromboli's the answer for me and for you.

Roll it, bake it, and share with glee,

It's Time to Eat
Stromboli

Stromboli's the meal for the whole family!

ABOUT THE CREATOR

Walter the Educator is one of the pseudonyms for Walter Anderson. Formally educated in Chemistry, Business, and Education, he is an educator, an author, a diverse entrepreneur, and he is the son of a disabled war veteran. "Walter the Educator" shares his time between educating and creating. He holds interests and owns several creative projects that entertain, enlighten, enhance, and educate, hoping to inspire and motivate you. Follow, find new works, and stay up to date with Walter the Educator™

at WaltertheEducator.com

www.ingramcontent.com/pod-product-compliance
Lightning Source LLC
LaVergne TN
LVHW052015060526
838201LV00059B/4042